LOVE SNACKS

Let's have a poetry party!!

Poetry by
WILLIAM BERTRAND

Illustrations by
FRANCES ENRIQUEZ

# FriesenPress

Suite 300 - 990 Fort St
Victoria, BC, V8V 3K2
Canada

www.friesenpress.com

Copyright © 2020 by William Bertrand
First Edition — 2020

Artwork by Frances Enriquez
Photograph of William on back cover by Angela Lee.
All other photographs by permission of owners.

All rights reserved.

No part of this publication may be reproduced in any form, or by any means, electronic or mechanical, including photocopying, recording, or any information browsing, storage, or retrieval system, without permission in writing from FriesenPress.

ISBN
978-1-5255-8802-0 (Hardcover)
978-1-5255-8803-7 (Paperback)
978-1-5255-8804-4 (eBook)

1. POETRY, CANADIAN

Distributed to the trade by The Ingram Book Company

In honor of Dad and Mom
and
the men and women working in Protective Services.

Let us be people of mercy
and share goodness with the people we meet.

Peace be with you.
And thank you very much for all your hard work and care.
Thanks be to God, parents and Family, priests and our
many friends
and helpers.

William Bertrand

Let's have a poetry party!

*Gather your family
Read some poetry
Enjoy some snacks
Play some classical music
Share happy memories!*

Part 1

Love Snacks Introduction

Life is like a great wedding reception
It all starts by saying hello
Many, many times
Soon we become friends!

We serve up Love Snacks
Like hot and cold hors d'oeuvres
We are in motion like a dance
Moving from room to room
Table to table and guest to guest
Making sure everyone is happy
We bring cheer to one another!

We are sharing in God's love
We are sharing in His love snacks
In childhood recreation…
Life at school and summer vacations
Family stories and the challenge of work
Even in God's great healing when we get sick

Yes, we too find healing with healthy words
And from the tree of life
This is amazing!

It is good that a friend learns from the tree of life
To con-forge, that is to learn from the heart
Slowly and laboriously over time
It is good that a friend learns from the tree of life
And shares this with their friends
And learns Wisdom and Understanding
From the full spectrum of humanity
Like a Rainbow... bringing hope to people

From childhood to dating
From marriage to bearing children
Single as I am, I too am bearing children
In the helping assistance that I bring

You will have to learn how to breathe
That is no formal breathing
That is no preaching
And expounding knowledge
From your great learning
From all of the books that you read
No, you will be sharing your own life
You will share your life with new friends
With a small spoon...
So, share your Love Snacks from the Tree of Life
And soon you will be the Host

LOVE SNACKS

To a wedding reception
Going from table to table
Welcoming your new friends

Going from care-home to care-home
Hospital to hospital
Social-service agency to social-service agency
Meeting new friends and sharing stories

My Dad likes appetizers of many kinds
Here is a banquet of Love Snacks for your enjoyment!

Topics for Discussion

How have you been enjoying your life?

Part 2

Children

They grow up fast
Who are those twelve-year-olds on the bus?
We stop at the university and they get off
These are university students
Am I ever getting old!

Our young adult group at church
Many who just graduated from university
Decided to put on a production of the musical Godspell
People auditioned for parts
The performance was entertaining, complete with musicians and crew
Youth sure can shine when given the opportunity!

It reminds me of a school play that I was in
It was a serious play and we had our parents' attention
The drama, right on the edge of your seat
Right at the climax of the play
I froze, hit my head with my hand, and said out loud,

WILLIAM BERTRAND

"Oh no, I forgot my lines!"
Our parents roared with laughter
I stumbled through my lines with no one hearing
And the play was over.

The Barbershop

One of the outings that we would go out for
Was a trip to the barbershop with Dad
We would have to sit on a board
Across the arms of the big barber chair and keep still
We did not want to get our ears clipped
Crew cuts were the style of the times by order of Dad

When I was a young man I still kept my hair short
And would go to the old-fashioned barbershop
It was operated by an old man who had to be in his eighties
While I was sitting in his chair
He told me a story about a young man getting his first shave
The young man kept saying, "What is this for, what is that for?"
With each application of hot towel, soap, and balm

The old man thought that it was quite an amusing story
And must have told it to lots of his clients
I sat back quietly, listening, enjoying the moment
Because the story was about me
When I went to him for my first shave six months ago

Topics for Discussion

Talk about a
childhood memory.

Part 3

A Heart of Gold

A ten-foot by ten-foot downtown room
With a mattress, fridge, hot plate, but no food
I share a bagged lunch with my friend
Lunch is a cheese sandwich, ripe banana, muffin, and juice
Which I bought for two meal tickets from the Mission
"Welcome to the club," he says

That same friend meets me on the street when I am
feeling lonely
He smiles at me like the rising of the sun
And asks me to take him out for coffee

It is good to have a friend with a heart of gold
Even when both of you don't even have five bucks to
your name

Stay in school, study, study, study!
Work, work, work!
Try to improve your employability!

WILLIAM BERTRAND

Heaven

Heaven is when you are really starving
And there is only a partial box of cereal in the cupboard
with no milk
Because your roommates drank it in the middle of the night
Then you go to a prayer group meeting
And there is a table full of sumptuous snacks and deserts
And you have not had a decent meal for days

Thank God for good food!

Heaven is when you are really starving for a day off
You have to work nine days with only one day off
That happens to be Christmas Day…but…
You have to work Boxing Day and that is really the Pits!

Then it happens to snow Christmas night
And drop four feet of that beautiful white stuff
All over the place
Shutting down the whole city for a week

Wow! I don't have to go to work!
Now that is Heaven!

WILLIAM BERTRAND

Part 4

Hockey

The game of hockey was a gift given to me by my parents
Dad flooded the backyard to make a small rink
And helped to teach me how to skate
Over the years I developed many friendships while playing hockey
Dad would drive me to games and practices
And encouraged me to hustle a bit more
I grew accustomed to losing games by large numbers
Even in senior hockey

One year I was on the traveling team in Bantam hockey
We would play two games per week
And would practice one day per week
With school I was very busy and would have to keep my grades up
Halfway through the season it happened
I was hit into the boards and broke my collarbone
I went to the bench crying; my hockey season was over

Dad took me to the hospital to get me bandaged up

After my doctor's appointment
Mom and Dad treated me to meals of pizza and
fried chicken
To cheer me up

For two months Dad would take me once per week to
watch my team play
Sometimes I would go to the dressing room to talk with
my teammates
They would ask me: when are you going to make
your comeback?
And in February I started to skate with the team
during practice
I did dress for one game near the end of the season
But my shoulder was still too tender
We made the playoffs
My coached dressed me for the last game
We won the Provincial Championship
And I was dressed in uniform to receive our trophy

After the season one of the parents had a party for our team
One of the mothers spoke words about each player
She said to me, "With a broken collar bone Bill's season
was short
But by staying with the team he has been a good sport."

Somewhere, in the difference between winning and losing,
is Grace

Part 5

Kitty Cats

My many friends all have different personalities
Like kitty cats
Most of my friends are quite shy
They have to be cared for and need lots of hugs
I know a few special friends that are like alley cats
They need lots of hugs too

I visited some seniors living in special care
We listened to some entertainers playing songs
And reminisced about the good old days
Of fishing, hunting, and working on the farm
A man told me that if you are watering the soil
You don't have to worry about the weeds
When you live in love and the soil is well watered
The weeds come out easily since they have not taken root
Love is brought about by bringing new friends to
old friends

One wise senior told me a secret in life
The mind lets you know what is in your heart
It is important to listen
Especially important is to listen for love
Not for money

I knew another friend who told me the same thing
He was my age but had bad experiences with some people
What he wanted was a true friend
We played some games of tennis that summer
Then he left town

Yes, some friends are like kitty cats and need lots of care
Maybe you will like to adopt one!

LOVE SNACKS

Intimacy

Fishing has a way of reviving the soul
Especially when it is with my best friend
Sitting on a bench
He is like a Maple Tree
Words come out slowly
After silent review
Bringing the unseen
More clearly into view
Like which way to go?
What is important in life?
What to keep?
What to let go?
We met through a common friend
Shared coffee for the first time
It takes time to get to know each other
We don't have to read the history of Israel
In one sitting
We are new wine for each other
I am blessed to have him for a friend

LOVE SNACKS

Topics for Discussion

How did you meet your best friend?

Why are you best friends?.

Part 6

Love Birds

It takes a long time to be a love bird
Love birds take a long time to learn love
Many nests they have built together
So careful with sticks and straw
Have you ever been a weaver?
I bet you have if you think about it
Too much work and the nest won't hold
Take time to weave in playful love

WILLIAM BERTRAND

Mother's Day

Wild flowers around a swampy lake
Small children among the flowers play
Paths emerge where little feet travel
And butterflies make for a playful chase
Tall flowers, short flowers
White, yellow, and blue
Three flowers picked even with roots
More than a handful for such tiny tots
Even prickly weeds are cherished
As mother loves every flower on Mother's Day

LOVE SNACKS

Topics for Discussion

How have your Mother and Father helped you?

Part 7

Philosophy

Ever think too much about a problem?
Ever stew too much and the pot gets burnt?
Sometimes philosophy is like chewing on a piece of black licorice
I realized this by observing a mother and a little girl
Her mommy said,
"Oh, you finished eating your licorice, let Mommy wash your hands and face."

Sometimes it is hard work being too much of an adult!

WILLIAM BERTRAND

Twinkle, Twinkle, Little Star

What gives you that twinkle in your eyes?
Could it be you are single and available?
Maybe you are happily married?
Could it be some sex appeal or zeal for life?
Could it be the thanksgiving you have for someone
Who has picked you up when you fell down?

It is a mystery to me!

To Be Love

How we shed light on each other
The gentle sun's rays
Cast radiance through the clouds and trees
I stroll down the lane
Like a skilled paintbrush
Shadows move silently
Revealing flowers of contrasting beauty
Cascading from the house's white walls
With ten steps the picture is gone
But leaves an imprint on my heart

May I be as gentle in passing…

No judging thought but to be love

WILLIAM BERTRAND

Part 8

Savior and Comforter

The Lord is my Savior and Comforter
Like young children
Sitting in front of the fireplace
With marshmallows to roast
And ghost stories told by an aunt
The Lord gathers the family together
And ignites the fire of love
Kindled with strangers
Of a people to call his own
Many times I thought before
Is it just us travelling all alone?
You have a big family, mother said
You just have not met them yet

WILLIAM BERTRAND

So we did meet
In the hour of gladness
In the hour of darkness
And in my new friends
We are becoming light

The Lord is my Savior and Comforter
As I sleep alone on a wet and stormy night

Part 9

Asking for Permission

I asked my Dad if I could go swimming with my friends
He said to go ask my Mom, so I did
And she said yes.

I asked my Dad if I could go to the baseball game.
He said to go ask my Mom, so I did
And she said yes.

I am starting to catch on
So one day I asked my Mom
If I could sleep over at a friend's house.

She said no.

So I asked my Dad
If I could sleep over at a friend's house.
He said to go ask my Mom.

I said, "I already did but she said no."
"Then what are you asking me for!" said Dad.
"I am the boss because your Mother said so!!"

Topics for Discussion

How do you
practice discipline?

What areas of life are you
interested in?

Part 10

A Hug

I feel that I have become a teddy bear
With lots of hugs over a cup of coffee
At my girlfriend's apartment,
About 2,500 cups in the past ten years,
Not including the Soup Kitchen or the Open Door.
A cup of coffee is the least expensive date you can go out for.
I have tried to go to the gym many times,
But that cup of coffee keeps calling me for a Hug!

Home

Crisp is the air we breathe
Twilight sleeping in the morning
The sound of bacon crackling on the Coleman stove
Our camp in the mountains, our temporary home
Breakfast is ready, out of our sleeping bags
A breathtaking view is our dining room
I see big-horned sheep on the neighbouring mountain
Clouds are our companion with an icy stream
We break camp, then on to the highway
To our next home.

Part 11

The Meaning of Life

One of the jobs that most people hate to do in the department store
Is to clean up and organize the ties around the round display tables.
It was such a monotonous job that I would make a game of it
By asking a few clerks to help out and have a tie party.
We would get together for the last half-hour before closing
To organize the ties and tell stories.
I told them, that if they would clean up the ties long enough
They would discover the meaning of life.

Months later, I was cleaning up the ties with a co-worker.
She was about twenty-six years old and was about six months pregnant.
All was quiet then she asked me,
"I wonder if my baby will have the same color eyes as my husband."

I said, "I told you that you will discover the meaning of life!"

Topics for Discussion

Talk about a "Great Discovery."

Part 12

Simplicity

I have said goodbye to many friends
And hello to many more
God's gift to us in human flesh
Was a story long ago
Now we live by the Spirit's breath
And the council of his word
This gift of life which I celebrate
Leaves me wondering even more

Of all the deeds which I have seen
Nothing can compare
To a life laid down in simplicity
In this fast-paced changing world
We are flooded with messages
That choke the gift of life
To enjoy each moment of life's gifts
As seasons come and go

Nature has its way of life
Trees know how to stand
The seagull's joy is in the air
Since long ago man has wished to fly
Why do things seem much more confusing now
In the hustling on the street
I throw it all like chaff into the wind
For a life of simplicity

LOVE SNACKS

Topics for Discussion

What do you have to let go of to reach your potential?

How can you develop your skills and talents?

Part 13

A Love Letter

Dear Friends!
Yes, it is good to pray for your friends
And make space for communion with them
Even if it is just an email or a phone call
A quick cup of coffee or even a hug
That is on a personal level
But why not invite God into the relationship too!
God loves to go out for a long walk with two friends in nature
And even sit on a park bench to listen for a while
To watch the squirrels play, the birds fly
And little children chase bunny rabbits
Yes, God is very active in the world
If we take the time to watch and listen:
As large as the rolling hills and the majestic sunsets
The moonlight at night and the creation of a new star
God is there, and also in the smallest of the small
God is in every insect, every blade of grass,

Every chemical reaction that takes place
Both inside and outside of the body
God is in it all!

He can speak every language
In every race of people
All mathematical, chemical, physical, biological formulas
In every combination
All of this which is seen or unseen
All of this takes place with the command of God
Isn't this very wonderful!!
Enjoy your day with God and your friends!!

LOVE SNACKS

Topics for Discussion

Talk about a beautiful day
that you had.

Part 14

God Blessed Me

God blessed me with a kind Mother and Father
My parents too were blessed with four sons
Two are married and now have children
This Christmas we will be together as one

Dad was raised to fish in moving waters
Hunt for birds among the marsh and reeds
The quiet times that we shared together
Companionship with sons a Father's creed

North to Alaska a song that I remember
Many times I visited my parents there
They showed me mountain streams and valleys
With glacier's timeless beauty with God's care

Winter-time was such a beautiful playground
With outdoor skating and forts of snow
Carnivals bring families together
And snowballing house to house we go

Lord you know how to furnish such a table
All creation is the work of your hands
Bless this day our parents with your goodness
And our priests that guide us with your command

Children learn to listen to your parents
That is what Grandma and Grandpa learned to do
Parents measure faith for your children's ears
And learn to read and love the Bible too

All that is left in life is to be a friend
A humble path for such a high calling
Let us seek those in need and bring good cheer
And be new wine when aged in golden years

Dad was raised to fish in moving waters
Hunt for birds among the marsh and reeds
The quiet times that we shared together
Companionship with sons a Father's creed

Part 15

1 Remember

I remember holidays, families and friends
Chinese food, the flavours blend
Swimming pools and summer heat
Camp in mountains was really neat
Family outings in the woods
Berry picking and home-baked goods
Blowing bubbles and play-fights
Niagara Falls, what a sight, what a sight

I remember fishing trips, off from school
With my Dad the golden rule
Climbing trees, sway in the breeze
With quiet moments, the Spirit breathes
Ocean waves, ten feet high
Nine miles out, my O my
We caught no fish in the swell
Learn to trust, I can tell, I can tell

WILLIAM BERTRAND

Who is that girl sitting over there?
The one with the brown and curly hair
Ever since our friendship grew
I'm so glad God gave me you
Wild meadows children play
Picking flowers for Mother's Day
Cherished gifts a wonderful bouquet
Father saves, He never throws away
Father saves, He never throws away
Father saves, He never throws away

Part 16

Where there is Sunshine

Where there is sunshine
And pure raindrops
There are rainbows
With the spoken word
From our Father
Through our shepherds
Leading onward
To our heavenly home

Where there is travel
Through troubled valleys
And we long for
The wine of the past
Winds of fire!
Rise up children!
Leading onward
To our heavenly home

Where there is hunger

But no food lacking
Give us freedom
From time that we waste
Share your bread in
New combinations
Leading onward
To our heavenly home

Where there are strangers
In a foreign place
Say the word "Hi"
New chapter of life
It's like new growth
In early spring
Leading onward
To our heavenly home

Let's come together
In the name of love
Plant a garden
With our own hands
Feed our neighbor!
With our friendship!
Leading onward
To our heavenly home

Where there is wonder
Wide wonderful love
Taste the champagne

LOVE SNACKS

With bubbly smiles
Holy Spirit!
Joy of Father!
Leading onward
To our heavenly home

Where there is sunshine
And pure raindrops
There are rainbows
With the spoken word
From our Father!
Through our shepherds!
Leading onward
To our heavenly home

Leading onward
To our heavenly home

Leading onward
To our heavenly home

Topics for Discussion

What are you hoping for in life?

How has opportunity been knocking on your door?

Where can you seek new opportunities?

Rowing your Boat

When we row our boat we use two oars and pull together, one on the left side and one on the right side. Navigating through life we have one oar in our domestic life and one oar in the institutional life. For life to be functioning and life-giving, we need the institutional life and the domestic life to both be functioning. My Dad and Mom received the Sacrament of marriage. They worked as a team and rowed the boat together, both pulling the weight. Dad worked in the military and Mom stayed home and took care of the home and the children. Dad was given the role by my Mom to handle the discipline; he had to deal with the stress of the institution while Mom was more of the quiet listening type. The weekend was for family time with lots of outings in nature. The best of our times was when we went as a family to church on Sundays, then went to the mess-hall for brunch, then for a country drive or picnic. However, when we were transferred we did not keep the Sunday practice. When my brother and I moved to Vancouver, Mom started to work, and I drifted away from church too.

In Vancouver I worked for a while in a den of vice, but my aunt later on would take me and my Grandmother to church. I did not participate in the Sacraments, I just listened. After church we would go to my aunt's house for lunch, then take Grandma back to the nursing home. I visited Grandma in the nursing home a few times, and she was very sad because hardly any of the family would visit her. Well, Grandma lived only a couple of years in the nursing home before she died. Her funeral was like Good Friday except it was not very good.

So with my volunteering for years with seniors in Victoria and witnessing unrequited love, I have come to the conclusion that to take care of seniors and the church we need the Institution Church and the Domestic Church both pulling their weight.

So what happens when we put too much emphasis on institutional life, be it church or work, and neglect the domestic life? I find that too much institutional life can end up with a person losing their humanity, becoming a silo of information, an instrument of production, a product. They feel like an "it," especially when there is no thanksgiving and the person ends up feeling used. It is in these situations that a person can feel trapped, with loss of dignity, and this effects the relationships around them. Jesus is the Good Shepherd and sees us in this situation, and he has ways of liberating us and restoring our dignity. Jesus takes away the yoke of slavery and gives us his yoke to wear: a yoke that leads us to refreshment and springs of healing, life-giving water. Jesus has ways of restoring family life and leading us home. Jesus does not want to be trapped, either: he does not want to be trapped in the Eucharist but to be given away. But Jesus is reserved in the tabernacle to be a Presence to help us when we are feeing trapped. Jesus wants freedom for us so that we come in and go out to find pasture and bring our presence to other people to enjoy rest in communion through friendship. And Jesus wants us to be a blessing for each other.

God is so gracious that when I lost the Sabbath while I was going to school and then I got sick, God gave me seven years of healing rest and care in a care home sanctuary and gave me many helpers. I see lots of people trapped in life, in the computer, internet, social media, lives of crime, addictions, debt, unhealthy relationships, isolation, etc.

One thing that I noticed while visiting with seniors is the benefit of sharing in their heritage, bringing to them a new springtime while learning how to worship in spirit and in truth. Seniors in a care facility are like an abandoned orchard. While sharing in their fruit, my tree too is growing little by little. I have found out that on those lonely days at home by myself, reading scripture prayerfully helps the roots to grow. Being renewed at church over and over and volunteering in the community is a way to give back to God and show Him our thanksgiving. It is good to feed from our heritage and inherit the Kingdom of God through love of neighbor.

After years of travelling to different places, one day I will be retired in a care facility, sitting in a rocking chair, and I will invite youth from various youth programs to visit and share their troubles with me so that I can cheer them up and bring some sunshine in their life. One of my regrets is that in serving the Lord and my Mom and Dad, I have neglected my three younger brothers. For this I need forgiveness. I was greatly blessed when I was far away from home but it will be another blessing to come back home and be a Holy Family loving each other just the way we are.

LOVE SNACKS

WILLIAM BERTRAND

It is the Mother and Father who visits their son
And cleans up his house when it is in disarray.

God's greatest work of Art is a family in Love
God bless our Parents for ever and ever!

Topics for Discussion

Write a song of thanksgiving for blessings you have received.

Frances Connell Enriquez

Frances was born in Miramichi, New Brunswick. She was National First Prize winner of the Brook Bond educational award at age 17. She then went to Europe and studied the great art of Paris, London and Rome.

She continued her advanced art training and education at the Instituto Allende in San Miguel, Mexico where she graduated with a MA in Fine Arts and at the Nova Scotia College of Art and Design where she obtained another MA in Art Education.

She spent many years teaching Art in Igloolik, NWT and Cape Breton and Antigonish, Nova Scotia. She has a BA, B Ed degrees from St. Francis Xavier University, Antigonish, Nova Scotia.

Frances traveled alone and with her husband Charles to many parts of the world and has sketched, painted, exhibited and taught art education in several locales including Nova Scotia, the Northwest Territories, India, Honduras, Mexico, Scotland, Sri Lanka, Malta, Italy and Australia.

For many years, she lived in Victoria BC where she taught and painted extensively. A significant experience at the All Saints of Alaska Orthodox Church in Victoria was the learning of Russian Iconography which opened a new and exciting world of Byzantine and Sacred Art for her.

In 2007, she returns to her place of birth, Miramichi, New Brunswick where she looks forward to new and creative forms of art expression. Besides her love of art, She enjoys circle dancing, knitting, fiddle music, red wine, Gregorian chant and contemplative prayer.

Her artistic statement is summed up in the Letter of Pope John Paul II to Artist.

"Every genuine inspiration contains some tremor of the "breath" which the Creator Spirit suffused the work of creation from the very beginning. Overseeing the mysterious laws governing the universe, the divine breath of the Creator Spirit reaches out to human genius and stirs creative power. He touches it with a kind of inner illumination which brings the sense of the good and the beautiful, and awakens energies of mind and heart which enable it to conceive an idea and give it a form of art. It is right then to speak, of "moments of grace", because the human being is able to experience in some way the Absolute who utterly beyond."

"Beauty is a key to mystery and a call to transcendence. It is an invitation to savour life and to dream of the future. ..It stirs that hidden nostalgia for God which a lover of beauty like St. Augustine could express in incomparable terms: Late have I loved you, beauty so old and new: late have I loved you."

"Beauty will save the world." F. Dostoyevsky

CPSIA information can be obtained
at www.ICGtesting.com
Printed in the USA
BVHW021330231220
595976BV00010B/101/J